COMMUNITY HELPERS

Counselors

by Kate Moening

BLASTOFF! READERS

BELLWETHER MEDIA · MINNEAPOLIS, MN

Blastoff! Readers are carefully developed by literacy experts to build reading stamina and move students toward fluency by combining standards-based content with developmentally appropriate text.

Level 1 provides the most support through repetition of high-frequency words, light text, predictable sentence patterns, and strong visual support.

Level 2 offers early readers a bit more challenge through varied sentences, increased text load, and text-supportive special features.

Level 3 advances early-fluent readers toward fluency through increased text load, less reliance on photos, advancing concepts, longer sentences, and more complex special features.

★ **Blastoff! Universe**

Reading Level

Grade **K**

Grades **1–3**

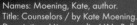

Grade **4**

This edition first published in 2021 by Bellwether Media, Inc.

No part of this publication may be reproduced in whole or in part without written permission of the publisher. For information regarding permission, write to Bellwether Media, Inc., Attention: Permissions Department, 6012 Blue Circle Drive, Minnetonka, MN 55343.

Library of Congress Cataloging-in-Publication Data

Names: Moening, Kate, author.
Title: Counselors / by Kate Moening.
Description: Minneapolis, MN : Bellwether Media, Inc. 2021. | Series: Blastoff! Readers: Community helpers | Includes bibliographical references and index. | Audience: Ages 5-8 | Audience: Grades K-1 |
  Summary: "Developed by literacy experts for students in kindergarten through grade three, this book introduces counselors to young readers through leveled text and related photos–Provided by publisher.
Identifiers: LCCN 2020029189 (print) | LCCN 2020029190 (ebook) | ISBN 9781644874004 (Library Binding) | ISBN 9781648342400 (Paperback) | ISBN 9781648340772 (ebook)
Subjects: LCSH: Counselors–Juvenile literature. | Listening–Juvenile literature.
Classification: LCC BF636.6 .M64 2021 (print) | LCC BF636.6 (ebook) | DDC 158.3–dc23
LC record available at https://lccn.loc.gov/2020029189
LC ebook record available at https://lccn.loc.gov/2020029190

Editor: Betsy Rathburn   Designer: Laura Sowers

Printed in the United States of America, North Mankato, MN.

Table of Contents

Maria had a fight
with her best friend.
She talks to
the counselor.

4

The counselor listens. She helps Maria decide what to do. Maria feels better!

What Are Counselors?

Counselors help people **handle** tough feelings. They work in offices and **health centers**.

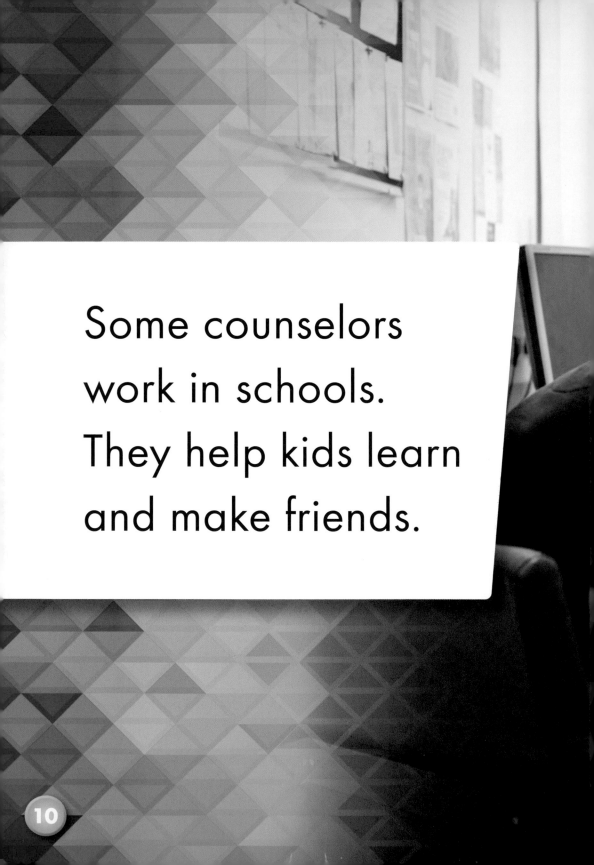

Some counselors work in schools. They help kids learn and make friends.

11

11

What Do Counselors Do?

Counselors help people face their problems. They ask questions.

Counselor Gear

desk   computer   chairs   phone

13

Counselors help people set **goals**. They help people make **decisions**.

School counselors help stop **bullying**. They want school to be safe and fun!

What Makes a Good Counselor?

Counselors listen well. They work hard to understand problems.

Counselor Skills

- ✓ good decision makers
- ✓ kind
- ✓ good communicators
- ✓ good problem-solvers

Counselors **communicate** well. They share ideas to fix problems. Counselors help people feel better!

Glossary

bullying

teasing or hurting
people to scare them

goals

things a person is
trying to do or finish

communicate

to share information

handle

to deal with

decisions

choices

health centers

places where doctors
and nurses offer
healthcare for people
in a certain area

To Learn More

AT THE LIBRARY

Leaf, Christina. *Teachers*. Minneapolis, Minn.:
Bellwether Media, 2018.

Manley, Erika S. *Counselors*. Minneapolis, Minn.:
Jump!, 2020.

Stratton, Connor. *Working at a School*. Lake
Elmo, Minn.: Focus Readers, 2020.

ON THE WEB

FACTSURFER

Factsurfer.com gives you
a safe, fun way to find
more information.

1. Go to www.factsurfer.com.

2. Enter "counselors" into the search box
   and click 🔍.

3. Select your book cover to see a list of
   related content.

Index